"At the beginning the Creator made them male and female, and said, 'For this reason a man will leave his father and mother and be united to his wife, and the two will become one flesh. So they are no longer two, but one.

"Therefore what God has joined together let man not separate."

—Matthew 19:4-6 NIV

"I DO"... WHAT?

An engaging look at the Wedding Vows, with
a discussion guide for pre-marriage counsel,
marriage enrichment, or small group studies.

DENNIS R. FULTON

WESTBOW
PRESS
A DIVISION OF THOMAS NELSON

WestBow Press books may be ordered through booksellers or by contacting:

WestBow Press
A Division of Thomas Nelson
1663 Liberty Drive
Bloomington, IN 47403
www.westbowpress.com
1-(866) 928-1240

ISBN: 978-1-4497-8317-4 (sc)
ISBN: 978-1-4497-8318-1 (e)
ISBN: 978-1-4497-8319-8 (hc)

Library of Congress Control Number: 2013901579

Printed in the United States of America

WestBow Press rev. date: 1/30/2013

TABLE OF CONTENTS

ACKNOWLEDGMENTS

First and foremost and above all, to my wife and typist, Wanda. My typing consists of the Columbus Method of "discover and land", or the Biblical method of "seek and you shall find". Wanda has been my typist since the days of college term papers. Without her skill, determination and insistence this book would never exist.

To Wanda, who has been patient with my attempts to perfect the "I do" and who has extended God's grace to me when I have failed.

To Wanda, the mother of our five children, grandmother to our fourteen, and great grandmother of eight and counting. She has partnered with me in sharing the contents of this book with our progeny.

To Rachel and Ruth, our daughters, with whom this material was shared in marriage counsel and who have encouraged their Dad to be an author as well as a preacher and teacher.

To Lauren, our granddaughter and her husband, Michael Martin, who are my most recent of hundreds of weddings. The miles between us interfered with pre-marital counsel, so they studied the manuscript of "I Do What" and recommended it being shared with others.

To Wendy Fitzgerald, Children's Minister par excellence ,from Tarpon Springs, Florida who read one of my first drafts. She suggested study notes would be helpful for pre-marital counsel and to be used in couples Small Group Studies for marriage enrichment.

I said first and above all, so finally to Wanda Fulton who has been wife, mother, grand and great grandmother and an example of the "I Do's" for over 60 years! What a woman! Thanks!

INTRODUCTION

"I Do"…What? What kind of title is that? And is there any possible need for such a book to be written, much less ever read?? To these two questions my answer would be, "I certainly think so." And this "think so" comes after a half-century of standing before couple after couple who were expected to answer "I do" to that question I was going to ask. Many times the couple standing before me was so exhausted they scarcely could comprehend the questions being asked. How could they begin to comprehend the depth of the answer they were giving? This exhaustion came, not just from the tension of the wedding, but from the weeks of preparation they had made for this momentous event.

Recently a little publication was given to me titled <u>Weddings</u>. Much of the publication consisted of advertisements from merchants who hoped to receive a slice of, what has become, a very lucrative business. They also published a checklist of wedding preparations that would be useful for any bride and groom. Useful, but thoroughly exhausting! There were 24 major procedures or events to be planned. Each of these called for decisions to be made. Many of these decisions would be freighted with possible conflict. Certainly so in some negotiations between the bride and groom, parents, siblings, their best friends, and some others who had no right to even offer an opinion. This 24 category checklist had 221 lines of information to be completed!!! Add to that the fact that in some families there are certain family members that do not cope well in the same room.

And they *all* are to be there at the same time and in the same place—this couple's wedding! The physical energy, alone, needed for the marathon of events leading up to the wedding make the Tour-de-France look like a bike ride around the block!

Then there is the wedding! "Did the flowers arrive yet?" "Is Mother okay? She did remember to take her nerve medicine, didn't she?" "Dad looks a little annoyed. I hope he will handle this calmly!" "I thought this was where the soloist was to sing the song we had chosen. Where is she? She *is* here, isn't she?" "Oh no, they can't get that candle to light…okay, okay, he did get it. They are all burning!" This litany goes on from one little incident to another.

Finally, yes finally, the groom follows the minister to the platform and the bride, in full bridal beauty, walks down the aisle. At last, "Dearly beloved, we are gathered together…" The ceremony has begun and soon they will answer "I do." And the minister will ultimately declare them to be "Husband and Wife!"

With the marathon of events leading up to the wedding, and the myriad of details of the ceremony, it seems unlikely that the bride and groom would be able to give attention to a single word spoken. What were those instructive and inspiring words spoken by the minister as he opened the ceremony? And what, down to every detail, were they asked to affirm? But they both, on cue, answered "I do" to that life changing question. Could there be a time in the days ahead that their innermost being would say, "*I do what?*"

That is the reason for and the purpose of this book. It is written with a prayer that the couple engaged to marry will be blessed by reading it well before their wedding. It is hoped that it will be read before the preoccupation of flowers, wedding attire, parents, honeymoon, or financial concerns have clouded the issue of what *really* is taking place in the ceremony. This book is being written with a heartfelt desire for you to have, not just a good wedding, but to have a great marriage.

P.S. A postscript in an introduction? Yes, I forgot to share with you a startling omission from that published wedding checklist. Nowhere in the "Must do's" was there a mention of a pre-marital counsel. Without a license or blood test you *could not* be married! And without pre-marital counsel you *should not* be married.

May this little book be a part of that marriage counsel. May it also serve as counsel to some couples who have long since said "I do," but are having a very tough time with the "doing." May there be some wisdom and experience in this book to help turn those rough days into "They all lived happily ever after."

S-h-h-h! The wedding is about to begin......

The Traditional Wedding Ceremony

Dearly beloved, we are gathered here in the sight of God, and in the face of this company, to join together this man and this woman in <u>Holy Matrimony,</u> which is an honorable estate instituted of God, signifying to us the mystical union that is between Christ and His church; which holy estate Christ adorned and beautified with His presence and first miracle that He wrought in Cana of Galilee, and is commended

of the Apostle Paul to be honorable among all men; and therefore is not to be entered into unadvisedly or lightly; but reverently, discreetly, soberly and, in the fear of God. Into this holy estate these two come now to be joined.

I. <u>HOLY MATRIMONY</u>

Marriage is holy matrimony. It is not some little game we cooked up on the side while God was away on a trip. And if He found out about our game, He certainly would not like the rules by which we play! Marriage is holy matrimony. It *was* and *is* God's *very good idea.*

God has some good ideas, doesn't He? Remember that almost unbearable, scorching summer day? You slipped your fried feet out of your skillet-hot shoes and stepped into that crystal clear, oh, so cool, stream that was flowing down the hillside. Crystal clear, cool water—what a good idea!

You had driven for hour after hour across, what had now become boring, table top land. But, then, a few little hills took the monotony from your drive. Could you ever imagine, though, the sight that awaited as you topped that next rise? There it was! A majestic mountain range with its snow-covered fingers piercing that azure blue sky!

Majestic mountains---what a good idea.

It was just about the most relaxing day you had ever experienced. Casually dragging you feet through the sun-warmed sand, you realized this beach continues as far as you can see! And that multi-shaded blue water, that rhythmically massages that beach, stretches farther than any eyes could begin to see. Oh, how relaxing and therapeutic! Warm sandy beaches—what a good idea!

Yes, God has many good ideas. That is what the Scriptures say in Genesis about God's creation. When He had called forth the light, God saw that the light was good. When He completed the land and the sea He saw that it was good. When He caused the land to produce vegetation, He saw that it was good. The fish and the birds—good. The animals—good. Genesis 1:27 says "So God created man in His own image, in the image of God He created him—*male* and *female* He created them."

Then a beautiful and amazing thing happens. The writer of God's Word had to add an additional word. All that God had made before had been "good". After the creation of man and woman God now declares it to be "*very good!*"

Marriage is God's very good idea—it is *holy matrimony*. So, before you make any response to the declaration of intent—or, certainly before you affirm the wedding vows, realize to whom your promise is being made. Marriage is from God and your "bottom line" promise is to God. Yes, there is a part of your promise that touches on the family of your beloved. In some ways you are promising to take care of their "little girl" or their "first-born son", but *your basic promise, is to God.* It will be a legally binding ceremony with the proper documents returned to the courthouse. You are making some promises to the civil authorities who issued the license, but *your basic promise is to God.*

Certainly, this very public ceremony is a deeply personal matter. No one, but the two who are standing "front and center," can fully grasp the flood of emotions as the "I do!" is declared. It *is* a personal promise between the two of you! But at the core of this promise is *the* promise you are making to God. This is *holy matrimony—God's very good idea!*

Declaration of Intent
This Woman This Man

John, will you have this <u>Woman</u> to be your wedded wife, to live together after God's ordinance in the holy estate of matrimony? Will

you love her, comfort her, honor, and keep her in sickness and, in health; forsaking all others keep only to her, so long as you both shall live?

Mary, will you have this <u>Man</u> to your wedded husband, to live together after God's ordinance in the holy estate of matrimony? Will you love him, comfort him, honor, and keep him in sickness and in health; and, forsaking all others, keep only to him, so long as you both shall live?

DECLARATION OF INTENT
II. THIS <u>WOMAN?</u> THIS <u>MAN?</u>

Will you, *John Quincy Smith*, take this woman, *Mary Ann Jones*, to be your wedded wife….keeping yourself to her only so long as you both shall live.

Will you, *Mary Ann Jones*, take this man, *John Quincy Smith*, to be your wedded husband….

The answer to this question is not the "I do" that will come later in the vows. This is the "I will" that declares your intention to wed. Of course, any couple standing in front of a minister, dressed in the finest wedding gown she could purchase, and in the best tuxedo he could rent, certainly intend to get married. In fact, this couple usually wish this uncomfortable hour could be ended so they can get on with the "they all lived happily ever after" bit.

Will they live happily ever after? That is their intent! Why, then, do so many end up in divorce court? It certainly was not their original intention. Who, but the few who regularly appear in the supermarket tabloids, ever stood up on that special day with a shrug and a "If it doesn't work out we can always divorce!" In a half-century of performing weddings I do not recall one where there was a half-hearted approach to their intention.

There is something about that "I will," however, that really must be understood before another step is taken toward the "I do." Most couples think that opening phrase is a clear intention of why they are getting married. I think, however, it is also one of the obvious reasons that couples are getting divorced! Double talk? No, hear me out by listening to the statement again.

Will you have this *woman?* Will you have this *man?* And therein lies the problem. This *woman*! This *man*! "No, that's not a problem—that's why we are getting married. We *are* heterosexual, you know." Yes, and that word hetero is exactly what I am addressing. Look it up in your collegiate dictionary. Hetero means *different*. Men and women are not alike! And that is one of the most overlooked causes of divorce!! That well-worn poster of yesteryear clearly pictures a difference. There they are, two cuties in their training pants. He, with the squat nose and deep dimples and she with that very thin, but oh, so cute, curly hair. They are both peering downward inside the front of their scanty wearing apparel. The title above the picture is "There is a difference!"

What a difference! The differences above the waistline, however, far exceed the differences below. There are many physiological differences, but there are also many psychological differences. Sure, some of these differences may have come from our culture. He was always given the football, and she was always given the baby doll. There are, however, some differences so basic that they did not come from the culture that surrounded them or the customs of the family that nurtured them.

There was a study of crib babies, not yet walking or talking, to observe any differences in their responses. As a toy was dangled before them, the boy babies showed a great interest in that toy. Most of the girl babies, however, showed a greater interest in the fingers that were dangling that toy. This certainly was not a cultural conditioning but was a basic and inherent difference. There were obvious and basic differences from the time the Scripture declared, "Male and female created He them." No, I am not talking superior or inferior, weaker or stronger, or good, better, and best—I am simply saying "different."

This *man?!* He will never, ever, if he lives to be a 100 years old, know what is involved in carrying a child within a womb. He will never give birth to a new life, even when it seems it may cost his life. He will never think like a woman, act like a woman, or react like a woman. He will never ever completely and totally understand her. So, how in the world is he going to share the rest of his life with her?

This *woman?!* You can just tell from looking at her that she is never going to be a man. How could she possibly understand what it is, even with the best of intentions, to be an agonizing spectator as the one he loves more than life ushers a new life into the world through blood and tears? No, she will never ever, be a man.

Women!?--"Why do they always have to cry? Why can't we just talk about this matter?" Men!?—"Why do they always have to be right? Why can't they just admit they made a mistake? Why in the world will he not stop and simply ask for directions?" Men? Women? They are different!! And that is where the burr under the saddle can get more painful the longer we ride. That is, unless we have squarely faced a problem about our human nature. The problem? Our human nature does not enjoy being around people who are different. I did not say *spiritual* nature or his *divine* nature. I did say, however, that our *human* nature does not enjoy the company of those who are different.

Why do you think there are racial tensions in the world? Economic box-outs? Social status? Unspoken caste systems or intellectual snobbery.

Yes, we all have some acquaintances and maybe a friend who is "*different.*" By far and large, though, we spend our time with people who like what we like. They enjoy doing what we do, going where we go, and talking the talk we talk. If someone steps too far outside these bounds the friendship begins to cool. Is this not a problem with you?

Do yourself a favor. Think back a few years ago to someone who was a friend, not just a casual friend but a cherished friend. As time passed, college, job relocation, or family breakup placed many miles between you. Now you were going to get to spend some time together! That first visit was exciting, but by the third or fourth outing together it became apparent the closeness was not there. "Well, they are different than they used to be." No, what you are really saying is "They are now different from me, and I just do not feel as close." So the friendship cools and could eventually end. Mad at them? Not at all, just no longer close. They are just different.

In the *declaration of intent* you are committing your life to some one, this *man* and this *woman*, who will always be different! Look for, celebrate, joke about, and enjoy that difference, even those differences that far exceed "viva la difference."

Declare your intention now! If you intentionally accept the sexual privilege of being different physiologically, you also intentionally accept the responsibility of being different psychologically. Will you have this *woman*? Will you have this *man?* Make it your intention to accept and celebrate those differences. There will be basic and obvious differences. Sometimes those differences will be absolutely delightful! But, there will be differences.

Declaration of Intent
This Woman, This Man

John, will you have <u>This</u> woman to be your wedded wife, to live together after God's ordinance in the holy estate of matrimony?

Will you love her, comfort her, honor and keep her in sickness and in health; and, forsaking all others keep only to her, so long as you both shall live?

Mary, will you have <u>This</u> man to be your wedded husband, to live together after God's ordinance in the holy estate of matrimony? Will you love him, honor, and keep him in sickness and in health; and forsaking all others, keep only to him, so long as you both shall live?

DECLARATION OF INTENT
III. <u>THIS</u> WOMAN? <u>THIS</u> MAN?

The declaration of intention contains a double barreled question, and it could result in a second explosion. Or, if properly considered, it could contain a second blessing. Let's take a second look at that declaration. What if the minister who presides at your ceremony were to ask, "Will you have <u>this</u> woman?" "Will you have <u>this</u> man?" Your minister will not ask the question in that manner, but what if he did? It is a different question and it calls for a different consideration of your intent.

What I am getting at? Years ago I had a very attractive couple sitting in my office making plans for their upcoming wedding. Not long after the marriage counseling sessions and the wedding planning meetings, I received a phone call from the would-be-groom to cancel the wedding. Everything had been "called off." You can imagine my surprise, then, when in a matter of months this would-be-groom was sitting in my office with a new potential bride. Would it have been out of order if I had asked, "Will you have <u>this</u> woman?" Am I overstepping when I say he could have answered, "Well, you know, she's not exactly the one I had in mind, but everything is going to be okay." Is this man alone in his thinking, or are the matrimonial woods full of suitors who believe everything will be okay. Okay, that is, after *they* have made a change or two in *their marriage partner.*

Since this mind-boggling event, I have made it a point in pre-nuptial counsel to discuss the <u>this</u> woman and <u>this</u> man emphasis in the declaration of intent. This woman whose hand you are holding right now! This man you are gazing at with those bright eyes right now! Not the man or woman he or she will be after all the subtle changes you hope to make in them. This man! This woman! Right here! Right now!

After years of counseling distraught couples, the loud explosion that comes from this part of the double barrel intention still surprises me. When we have worked our way through all the blame placing, all the responsibility dodging, and the frequent name calling, we realize that they are dealing with a problem they knew they had even before they married. I could throw my hands up in the air and shout, "Why in the world did the two of you get married anyway?"

The hands have never gone up and the shout has never yet come, because I know why they married. They believed "After we are married, he/she will change." " I knew he was drinking too much, but I was sure that would change after the wedding." "I knew she loved to shop, but I thought this credit card thing would stop when we bought a house" "I knew he liked to spend a lot of time with his buddies, but I thought that would let up when we could be home together in the evenings"…"I knew she had an explosive temper, but I thought that would change after we had children."

Do I need to go on in these, not-so-make-believe, conversations? Or, do couples need to take an honest look before they marry?? It takes a lot of faith, hope, and love to marry. But, as much as anything, it takes a lot of *honesty*. Is there a problem before you are married? Can you openly and honestly discuss this problem? If not, you had best not kid yourself. It will not be better or easier to talk about this after you are married. This man and this woman are very much a part of the marriage formula.

Oh yes, there can and there will be changes! They will come when they come through the one who wants to change, not through the one who wants to *make* them change. Understand this—people do change. In fact, people like change! Do I need to say that again? I will!! People like change. It almost needs to be said a third time to counter all the baloney we have been fed. That baloney is labeled "People don't like change." It's still baloney any way you slice it.

People like change!!! Just listen to the excitement as they tell about their job change. Watch them climb out of that new car and look around to see who is watching. They are just waiting for an opportunity to show you all the new gadgets. And, isn't that a different cell phone than the one you just bought six months ago? New clothes, new house, new phone, and just wait till you hear where we are going on this next vacation.

People like change! What people *do not* like is someone manipulating or *forcing them to change.* Church leaders would do well to keep this in mind. And those who stand inside those church buildings on their wedding day would do well to keep that in mind! There will be changes—delightful and meaningful changes. They will come, however, through love, loyalty, and maturity. They will not come because you try to change your bride or groom. He will cease being a couch potato only when he is sick and tired of his flabby potato skin. And she will only lose weight when she really desires to change her appearance and her health. Anything other than this takes that which God designed to be beautiful *companionship,* and turns it into terminal, combative *competition*!

In the meantime, will you have this man just as he is? If not, why eight years and three children later make that decision? Or will you have this woman? If not, leave her alone and some fellow will come along and find she is exactly what he wanted. And they, out of love, loyalty, and maturity, will come to those almost unnoticed changes that lead them to "live happily ever after".

<u>The Marriage Vows</u>
<u>For Better For Worse</u>

I, John Quincy Smith, take you Mary Ann Jones to be my wife, to have and to hold, from this day forward; <u>for Better, for Worse,</u> for richer for poorer, in sickness and in health, to love and to cherish till death do us part. And according to God's holy ordinance, I promise you my love.

I, Mary Ann Jones, take you, John Quincy Smith to be my husband, to have and to hold from this day forward; <u>for Better for Worse,</u> for richer for poorer, in sickness and in health, to love and to cherish, till death do us part. And according to God's holy ordinance, I promise you my love.

IV. <u>FOR BETTER FOR WORSE</u>

Who has not yet heard the old joke? The mountain preacher asks Zeke "For better or for worse?" And Zeke answers "Better!"..."For richer and for poorer?" And Zeke answers "Richer!"..." "Sickness and in health? And the answer is "Health!" That's a joke?? If it is, the joke is on Zeke. It is not a multiple choice question. There is a conjunction in there and there is no choice! The choice is "I do!" or "I don't". The "I don't" means there is a refusal of your marriage vows. The "I do" means it's a done deal on your part. It is for better and for worse.

Yes, it will be better! I promise you there are those things that will be better. Some things are just better together...peaches and cream...warm cookies and cool milk...fruit and cereal...man and woman. In fact, that's how those two started out in the beginning... together. Adam said "she is bone of my bone and flesh of my flesh." Without a knock at singleness or without the slightest depreciation of any individual, I will have to say there are some things that are better if shared in marriage. I do not mean *just sex*. I do mean sex, but I do not mean *just sex*. There are many things in life that become better when shared in a meaningful, unselfish, and loving relationship. They are part of that *"very good"* that God declared when He created man and woman.

Just as I promise there will be those things that will be better than expected, I can promise you there will be some things that will be worse. I do not know what they will be in your marriage, but I promise you there will be. There were for Wanda and I, for my mother and father, for my grandparents, for my great grandparents. There were some things that were "worse" for Adam and Eve!

That "worse" part is covered in your marriage vows. The problem is, how much worse are we talking about? The word is *worse*, not *worser*. There is no such word as *worser*. The word is worse and it is an open ended word. The danger comes when we place our own preconceived limits on this word. Those limits usually come from some inordinately bitter marriage experiences of a friend or family. "If she would ever do to me what Sylvia did to Carl, it would be over!"…"If he, even once, did to me what Joe did to Crystal, I would end the marriage that day."

We know that there are clauses in the scripture that allow the dissolution of marriage. Those scriptures do not demand a divorce, but they certainly do allow it. Marriage has clearly been ended in the death of a spouse. The Bible also says for fornication (why the word adultery was not used, I do not know) a divorcement may be given. Paul, in I Corinthians 7, declares that a married brother or sister is no longer "bound" if the unbeliever refuses to live with them because of their Christian convictions. In all these cases divorce is not demanded, but it is certainly permitted!

Let me suggest, however, that the only couples that make it are those who have determined that nothing, absolutely nothing is going to stop their marriage. By *make it,* I do not mean they are like two pugnacious bulldogs, each holding on to their end of a rope, while snarling and growling at each other every day. I do mean those who make it to that "better" part of marriage are the ones who have pre-determined that nothing is going to interfere with their marriage. When a problem turns up, large or small, they *know* what they will do with their marriage. They only have to concentrate on what they will do with their problem. Anything less than this understanding of "for better and for worse" only leads to unanswered problems and suspicion about your marriage. Problems that are left unsolved become "worse" today than they were yesterday. And the next year will become a "lot worse" than the year before. It finally reaches the "*that's worse_enough—no more for me*" stage. Those whose vows of "better or worse" included the "worse than we expected" part will become those who experience that which is "better than we could have ever imagined" part!

The Marriage Vows
For Richer For Poorer

I, John Quincy Smith, take you, Mary Ann Jones to be my wife, t to have and to hold, from this day forward; for better for worse, <u>for Richer for Poorer,</u> in sickness and in health, to love and to cherish, till death do us part. And according to God's holy ordinance, I promise you my love.

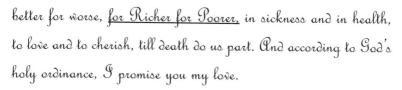

I, Mary Ann Jones, take you, John Quincy Smith to be my husband, to have and to hold from this day forward; for better for worse, <u>for Richer for Poorer,</u> in sickness and in health, to love and to cherish, till death do us part. And according to God's holy ordinance, I promise you my love.

V. <u>FOR RICHER FOR POORER</u>

If statistics are to be trusted, well over half of the divorces in America have money problems at their core. That has not been my experience in counseling. I can see, though, that many primary problems in a marriage could certainly result in money problems in the home. Above all, I can see that this part of the marriage vows best be taken into account.

A marriage is the union of two people. It is also the union of two financial backgrounds. These two backgrounds may be radically different. One of these potential newlyweds may have come from a home where George Washington was a cherished friend. Every time he showed up he was plunked into a bank and kept forever. The other family may have a different view of George. Every time he showed up they ran to the Dairy Queen and George was licked to death.

Yes, these are financial extremes! And ridiculously so! It would be hoped, then, that the new couple will differ from these ridiculous extremes. They should not, however, be too different from each other in this practical matter. How well do you know your potential lifetime financial partner? How important are "things" to them? Are they into saving? Or into spending? Can you truly say you know this man you are marrying? Does he have enough ambition to make a lasting partnership? "All he ever does after work is to crash on that couch and watch television Baseball! Basketball! Football!! Anything that bounces! I want more out of life than that. He has absolutely no goals and no ambition in life."

There are other men, however, with *too much* ambition. The

wife doesn't have a husband! He walks like a husband, talks like a husband, smells like a husband, but he is not a husband. He is a success machine. He's out to "make it!" and "If you don't make it by the time you are 40 you don't make it!" And this man is really making it

Consequently, his children will not have a father, but they will have an overload of things!!! Look in their bedroom! Open the double doors to that overcrowded closet, if you dare! And wow, what is that in the driveway on their 16th birthday? No father! No husband! Just too much ambition and lots and lots of things.

How well do you know this woman? Is she a mink-coat-girl or a cotton-coat girl? I don't mean which does she have. I mean what is her very strong preference? Some girls would not wear a mink coat if you gave it to them. Others? It would be the only thing they would wear if they could get their hands on one. And, what kind of house does she eventually want. Yes, out of her love for you she may start out in a rather dingy apartment, but what does she really want?

I have heard it said that a doctor does not have to wait for a baby to be completely born to tell if it is male or female. As soon as the head appears in the birth canal he knows. If there is a floor plan on the crown of the head he says, "It's a girl!"

Do you know the floor plan stamped on her head and in her heart? And is his ambition level pathetically low or dangerously high? Or is it just right? Remember that your marriage, like it or not, will be for richer or for poorer. Why not some honest discussion about how important *things* are to the two of you? Or are *things* important at all? That discussion could well be one of the best investments you will ever make toward your future together

The Marriage Vows
In Sickness and in Health

I, John Quincy Smith, take you Mary Ann Jones, to be my wife, to have and to hold, from this day forward; for better for worse, for richer poorer, <u>in Sickness and in Health,</u> to love and to cherish, till death do us part. And according to God's holy ordinance, I promise you my love.

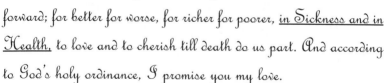

I, Mary Ann Jones, take you John Quincy Smith to be my husband; to have and to hold, from this day forward; for better for worse, for richer for poorer, <u>in Sickness and in Health,</u> to love and to cherish till death do us part. And according to God's holy ordinance, I promise you my love.

IV. IN SICKNESS AND IN HEALTH

That hand you will be holding as you state this vow is attached to a body—a physical body. And physical bodies, at any given time, can either be sickly or healthy. There is not much in between! Guess what? This part of the vow is probably going to be put to the test before "better or worse" or "richer and poorer." It could well be put to the test on your honeymoon. With the stress of all the preparations and the marathon of activities leading up to your wedding, you would not be the first couple to return from a honeymoon that has been tinged by the misery of bride or groom, or both, experiencing sickness rather than health.

It could be, however, that this part of your vows may not be put to the immediate test. You certainly could have a honeymoon that is even more than you had dreamed. But, if health is not immediately tested, this part of the vow could certainly be the ultimate test of your devotion.

Who doesn't blanch at the words "early dementia" "cancer" "stroke" or "crippling disability"? And who does not think of the devotion needed when the doctor has uttered one of these words about your mate? We know and they know that the ultimate test has begun. The diagnosis, though, may not be this harsh. It may be less than one of the ultimate tests. It may simply be the daily test of chronic disease, lupus, diabetes, asthma. Or it could be an almost endless list of day-by-day illnesses.

In sickness and in health has a definite bearing on the day-by-day life around the house. It obviously has an impact on what happens in the bedroom at night. Sex, if it is all that God designed it to be, is an "in health" event. If not loaded with the guilt of an illicit, darkened quarters of a motel, or the back seat of an automobile, sex is physical, mental, emotional, and spiritual. It is an all consuming event and it is not easily achieved by those who are less than well.

Many have been the times that the poor health issue has contributed to or been the cause of sex outside of marriage. "I don't know what's wrong with her" he said in a personal counseling session. "She's always laying around on that couch, always tired, and always complaining. And there is this girl at the office! She's bubbly! She's lively! And we didn't mean for anything to happen. We really didn't." This counseling conversation has often been repeated. A different artist and slightly different lyrics, but basically the same old song.

This same old song was sung to me by the wife of a policeman who was a gigantic specimen of manhood. Her words, however, painted a different portrait. "I have known him to stay in bed for three whole days. Other than meals or the bathroom, he simply lays around in that bed!" Seventy-two hours!?! Fortunately for that clod (can I use that word?) his wife was strongly committed to Christ. Had she not have been, the "sickness and health" vow would have withered on the vine. Without her steadfast prayer life, I would not have been surprised to have received a phone call saying. "There's this man two blocks down the street. We've known each other for sometime...and yada, yada, yada." So goes the rest of another sad story about sickness and health.

Hold tightly to that hand during the vows and every day after the wedding. It is attached to a physical body that is subject to sickness and health, just as is the body of the hand they will be holding! Thankfully, you, and they, have wisely covered this matter in your marriage vows when you promised "in sickness and in health."

The Marriage Vows
I Promise You My Love

I John Quincy Smith, take you Mary Ann Jones to be my wife, to have and to hold, from this day forward; for better for worse, for richer for poorer, in sickness and in health, to love and to cherish, till death do us part. And according to God's holy ordinance, <u>I Promise you My Love.</u>

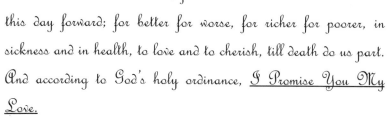

I, Mary Ann Jones, take you John Quincy Smith to be my husband, to have and to hold, from this day forward; for better for worse, for richer for poorer, in sickness and in health, to love and to cherish, till death do us part. And according to God's holy ordinance, <u>I Promise You My Love.</u>

VII. <u>I PROMISE YOU MY LOVE</u>

In the old days the conclusion of the vows was "And thereto I plight thee my troth." But what in the world does that mean?

Many ministers, then, have changed that conclusion to "I promise you my love." But what does that mean? We have done such a number on the word *love* that it can mean almost anything, can't it? "Oh, I would love to live in a house like that"..."Man, oh, man I'd love to have a big 4WD pickup truck"..."I just love pina coladas"..."I love fresh Dutch apple pie"..."Yeah, and I love homemade lemon pie with meringue about that thick."

Then, there are those cheap and cheapening paperback novels that vividly describe what they call "making love." But the very graphic actions they describe in this process can be carried out by two horses in the middle of the pasture. It did not begin or end with love. It was only an instinctive breeding process, and that was all!!

After the damage we have done to the word *love*, it is almost confusing to read "God so loved the world that He gave His one and only Son, that whoever believes in Him will not perish, but have eternal life." Loving a house? A car? A pie? Making love? And, God so loved? What does this word '*love*' really mean?

We have to admit that when we use the word *love*, we really mean *like*. I like that house! I like that car! I like lemon pie! When the Bible uses the word it has a deeper and truer meaning. God did not "so like" the world that He gave his one and only son. In fact, He did not like what He saw in me at all, but He loved me enough *to do* something about it. We, however, keep on using the word *love* when we really mean *like*, and especially when we want to describe how we *feel* about something. In our culture, love is not an action. It is a feeling. *And therein is a huge problem.*

Unless we come to understand this concluding statement in our wedding vows, we will ultimately come to the conclusion of our marriages.

Many couples have sincerely, but genuinely, lied to each other as they concluded their vows. They did not intend to lie, but they did. If they were promising a love that is defined by their culture, they promised a lie. If love, to them, is some kind of special feeling, they just promised a lie! How can anyone in the whole wide world promise how they will *feel* five years from now? Even next year for that matter? Or, the day after the honeymoon? You *cannot* promise how you will feel. So, what are you promising when you say "I promise you my love?"

The answer is in that "God so loved" kind of love. It is the kind of love described by the apostle Paul in I Corinthians 13. He defines love by what *you do*, not by what you *feel*. And with God's help that kind of love *can* be promised in your vows. He says love is *patient*, so "I promise, with God's help, I will be patient with you." Love is *kind,* so "With God's help, I will be kind to you". *Love does not envy.* "With God's help, I will not be jealous". Love is *not boastful…not proud…not rude! Not, selfish…not easily angered!* With His help, these promises can be fulfilled. You are not promising how you are going to *feel.* You are promising what you are going *to do* when you vow "I promise you my love."

What about the feelings, then? Let me make you a promise. And in that promise there is really good news. That promise? The promise is "The *feeling* comes from the *doing*—and not the other way around."

Be patient with me a minute. Let me try to illustrate that promise. What if we were to find out that one of our sons was not really our son? What if the nurses in the OB ward in Winston-Salem, North Carolina, had really blown it big time. The wrong male baby had been brought to Wanda after his first hours in the nursery!! He's not our son! Our real son is some beach-bum in Malibu, California. It would be confusing, but do you think our feelings for the one we called our son all these years would cease to exist? No! He's the one with whom we had some sleepless nights during his childhood... we survived those teen years together...his was the diagnosis of Hodgkin's disease and the year of treatments to battle the cancer. No, the *feelings* would not be gone! We had shared too much *doing* over the years. But what about that Malibu beach bum? What would our feelings be toward him? At best, our *feelings* about him would remain confused until there had been some time of *doing* for him.

Am I making a point? Let me stretch it even further. I think the <u>doing</u> can even develop our *feelings* toward inanimate objects. For example, think of the house in which you live. You return from vacation and as you pull into your driveway there is that "Good to be home" feeling. Home? It's just a house, isn't it? If you are in a large subdivision there are dozens of houses with exactly the same floor plan. Even the driveways and the garage doors are identical! Why do you have feelings toward this house? Why not drive up to the identical house down the street and have that "Good to be home" feeling? Well, "See that tree in the back yard? I planted that tree! Those gutters? I replaced them myself! Look at those flowers... the lawn...the patio in the back." The litany goes on and on and demonstrates my point. Our feelings for that house come from all that has been done for and in that house. Feeling for an orderly pile of building materials? Those feelings came from the doing? You bet!

And what about your feelings toward that car? You know, the used one you bought in college. The same one you later used for a second car. You ran the wheels off of it—kept it until it became a bucket of rusty bolts. Then, you finally traded it in on a new car!!! Two weeks later you drive past a used car lot and there it is—your car! And guess what? There were feelings that surfaced as you looked at "ole faithful!" Feelings? It's just a car. General Motors only made 112,000 just like it. In fact, a fourth of them were painted the same color as yours. Feelings? "Yeah, that's the car we were driving when

I hit that patch of black ice. We spun around three times and barely missed a huge oak tree. Talk about a heart-thumping trauma! And I can never forget the intense labor my wife was having! We did not make it to the hospital in time! Our second child was born in the back seat of that car." Feelings? You bet! Feelings for that well worn jalopy because of all the doing during the time you owned it.

I can make you a money-back offer. The *feelings* come from the *doing* and not the other way around. When a man walks into my office and, after running conversational circles, finally says to me, "I just don't feel like I love her anymore", I guarantee you he, a long time before, had stopped doing for her all those things he was doing when he was trying to impress his future bride. The doing has ceased and, as to be expected, the feeling has died.

Clearly understand, then, the *doing* is what you are promising in these last five words of the wedding vows. You dare not be trapped by your culture into believing you are promising the *feelings* you have on your wedding day. If you do, your vows will be a lie! You cannot promise how you will feel in the future!! What you are promising is what you will be *doing* from this day forth. Read, again and again, I Corinthians 13:4-7. That is what you will be promising, and, with God's help, that is what you will be doing. And the *doing* will take care of the *feeling*. I promise! I promise, too, that this ' *doing*' is what leads to the "Happily ever after!"

Presentation of the Rings

Having presented this token as a seal and and as a remembrance of the vows you have made, will you place this ring on her finger and repeat after me:

<u>With this ring I thee wed</u>; in the name of the Father, and of the Son, and of the Holy Spirit. Amen.

Having presented this token as a seal and as a remembrance of the vows you have made, will you place this ring on his finger and repeat after me:

<u>With this ring I thee wed</u>; in the name of the Father, and of the Son, and of the Holy Spirit. Amen.

VIII. <u>PRESENTATION</u> OF THE RINGS

With this ring, I thee wed! A ring? Nothing too unusual about that. For centuries a ring has been used as the seal of the pledge made in the marriage vows. It certainly seems the perfect symbol for the pledge. Many a minister has pointed out that this perfect circle, as does love, has no end. Faith and hope may come to an end when they reach that place called sight. But love?? Love never ceases!

It could just as well be mentioned that, just as there is no end to that circle, neither can you find the place when it began. It would be a challenge to most couples to tell exactly when their "marriage kind of love" began. I don't mean the first time they ever laid eyes on each other...or the very first date they had...or when they felt they were "falling in love"...or when they were pretty certain "this is it". What I mean is, at what split-second did you positively, beyond a shadow of a doubt, know this is the one with whom you wanted to share the rest of your life? Like that perfect circle, it's not that obvious where the circle begins. And it certainly is obvious that the circle has no ending! The ring you give on your wedding day is the pledge of a love that is, from this day forth, without end!

"Place this ring on her finger and repeat after me." Where else, dunce-like Minister, would you place the ring except on her finger. Where else? Well, there are still a few subcultures in the world where the ring is placed in her nose. In her nose as you would in the nose of a prize heifer, to be led about wherever her owner desires! Wise is the groom who remembers he is placing the ring on the finger of a hand that has *willingly* reached out to form a life-time partnership with him.

Even wiser is the one who places a deeper meaning to the presentation of this ring. The Scripture teaches the husband is to "Love his wife as Christ loved the church and gave himself up for it." His pledge of this kind of unselfish love will bless his bride each day of her life. Every time she looks at that ring surrounding her finger, she should know there is someone who is surrounding her life with his love. That was his pledge.

She, too, brings a ring on the wedding day. This has not always been the custom. For many years and in many cultures it was only the bride who wore a symbol of marriage. In fact, you have probably seen pictures of an Eastern bride with a strand of coins circling her head. For beauty? Yes, but also the symbol of her marriage. Seeing this picture in an anthropology publication gave me a whole new understanding of a story in the Bible. Remember the story of the woman and the lost coin? I know this story could have been set against a background of poverty, but, even then, I had difficulty in understanding why she would search diligently, tirelessly, endlessly until she found it. It became even more difficult to understand why the entire community would join in a "jump up and down" celebration because she had found her coin??

What if that coin, however, had been a part of the wedding strand that had been placed upon her head? A strand from which the Elders of the village would pluck a coin to disgrace a wife who was disrespectful or unfaithful to her husband! This woman was a faithful wife! Everyone in the village knew of her faithful love. The coin had fallen from its place accidentally! It was now found and could be restored to that strand that declared her love. It had been restored before her husband returned from his distant journey or his field of labor. Why not "jump up and down" at such a fantastic ending to a great story of faithful love?

I think that the coin in Jesus' story *was* a marriage symbol. No, I cannot be certain of that. I would hope, however, that every bride and groom would be certain of the meaning of the tokens that they present at the end of their ceremony. The ring she wears is the seal of his sacrificial love that will surround her life from this day forth. And the ring he is wearing is worn in confidence of her love that will be faithful and respectful from this day forth.

Proclamation of Marriage

In as much a these two have this day pledged their love before God and you and have sealed that pledge by the rings they have presented, each to the other; I declare to you by the authority of the governing state, and by the higher authority of the Word of God, that they are now <u>Husband and Wife.</u> What God has joined together, let not man put asunder.

You may kiss your bride!

Now, may I Introduce to you

Mr. and Mrs. John Quincy Smith

X. PROCLAMATION OF MARRIAGE

At this point the bride and groom stride joyfully down the aisle to be met by a shower of rice, birdseed, or bubbles—and to soon discover they are no longer bride and groom—they are now *husband* and *wife!*

There were some final words, however, after *husband* and *wife*. Those words were *"What God has joined together, let not man put asunder."* That well-known phrase was spoken by Jesus when He was commenting on marriage. The complete statement He made was "Have ye not read that He which made them in the beginning, made them male and female and said 'For this cause shall a man leave father and mother and cleave to his wife, and they twain shall be one flesh.' Wherefore they are no more twain but one flesh. What therefore God hath joined together let not man put asunder." Matthew 19:4-6 KJV

One of the great challenges for every couple will be the *leaving, cleaving, and uniting.* How they respond to these three words will determine those other words—*"and they all lived happily ever after.*

After this chapter, I will present some thoughts that I believe will help with the *happily ever after.* The chapter that follows is not an *add-on.* It is the essence of what the author of marriage tells in *His* book. Neither is this chapter an *after-thought.* It comes from the forethought of the Holy Spirit in writing to those who would preserve their marriage, even in the midst of a promiscuous, sex-saturated culture.

The original words written in Ephesians 5 were to those who lived in such a culture in First-Century Ephesus. In the forethought of the Holy Spirit through the Apostle Paul, they were also written to *every* husband and wife living out their marriage in the 21st Century.

Biblical Blueprint for Marriage

Ephesians 5:21-33 "Submit to one another out of reverence for Christ. <u>Wives, submit to your husbands</u> as to a the Lord. For the husband is the head of the wife as Christ is the head of the church, His body of which He is the Savior. Now, as the church submits to Christ, so also wives should submit to their husbands in everything. <u>Husbands, love your wives,</u> just as Christ loved the church and gave Himself up for her to make her holy, cleansing her by the washing with water through the word, an to present her to Himself as a radiant church, without stain or wrinkle or any other blemish, but holy and blameless. In

this same way husbands ought to love their wives as their own bodies. He who loves his wife, loves himself. After all, no one hated his own body, but he feeds and cares for it, just as Christ does the church, for we are members of His body. For this reason a man will leave his father and mother and be united to his wife, and the two of them will become one flesh. This is a profound mystery, but I am talking about Christ and the church. However, each one of you also must <u>love his wife</u> as he loves himself. And the wife must <u>respect her husband</u>."

XI. __BLUEPRINT FOR__ __MARRIAGE__

Let's begin with the response and responsibility of the wife. I begin there, not because I am a male chauvinist. Not even because my father taught me to "open doors for a lady," "Never step in front of a lady," "Ladies first always." I start there because this scripture begins and ends with the wives. These same scriptures will, in turn, call the husbands to stand at attention and give account of their responsibility. Husbands next, but ladies first!

The verse that says "wives submit to your husbands as to the Lord," is surely an attention getter for both husband and wife. It is especially so in the KJV translation that reads "Wives be in subjection to your husband". His attentive response is "Yeah!" Hers is, "No way!!" Before the cheering becomes too loud and turns to a shouting match, let me have your attention for just a minute. You see, the word *submit* does not even appear in verse 22 in the Greek Scripture text. It is a part of that sentence that begins in the preceding verse. That is the verse that says, *"Submit yourselves one to another* out of reverence for Christ". There is a submission on the part of both husband and wife! If the idea of submission does not fit into your vocabulary, you should, under no circumstance, enter into a marriage. If you like your coffee the way *you* like your coffee…your room kept the way *you* want your room kept…your car treated in the way *you* treat the car—then *stay single*! And you can keep on doing everything in the manner in which *you* have always done it. And you can do it that way the rest of your lonely life. If it is marriage you want, however, some of the preferences that were always *yours* must eventually meld into *ours*. That is what submission to one another is all about.

In this passage of Scripture we are given a Biblical blueprint for marriage that is dependent upon submission "one to another out of reverence for Christ." It is the only blueprint that builds a structure strong enough to withstand the tests that come to marriages. How can any marriage survive in a culture where divorce is so easy and so frequent? It's a tough time for marriages, isn't it? But is it tougher *now* than for the people to whom this scripture was first written?

Could a Christian marriage survive in the pagan city of Ephesus? The patron goddess of that city was Diana, or Artemis, as she was called in the Greek culture. The temple to Diana in the city of Ephesus was one of the seven wonders of the ancient world. That temple had been destroyed, but had been rebuilt by the time the Apostle Paul wrote to Ephesus. That rebuilt temple and the worship of the goddess, Artemis, was the focal point of the city. Archaeologist have recovered many statues of the goddess. The entire top of her torso was covered with what appeared to be breasts. This multi-breasted goddess was the symbol of fertility! And her worship? Some scholars believe that on the holy days, hundreds of temple priestesses would go to the city to find the men who would share in the rituals. Then, in that pagan temple, they would enter into that which was scarcely a cut above a sex orgy. If that is worship, what is sin? How could marriage survive in such a culture? It was a culture where a family deemed it an honor for a daughter to be chosen as a priestess. It was a token of honor when a wife would, for a season, serve in the temple.

It was a culture where it was normal for a husband to go to the temple for daily rituals, if he desired. How in the world would a one-man one-woman commitment ever survive in that culture? How? By coming to the Biblical blueprint for marriage that would assure a structure so strong it could withstand the influence of Artemis in Ephesus! That same blueprint can also withstand the influence of Hollywood in the USA!

The *foundation* of a lasting marriage is that phrase, "out of reverence for Christ." The *building materials*, brick upon brick and board upon board, is the "submit to one another." Anything less than this will not be a lasting pattern.

The question, then, must be, "What blueprint will we follow?" You may have your heart set on a bi-level house, but if you have mistakenly followed the blueprint for a duplex, you will have a duplex. Kick, scream, or enter a lawsuit, you will still have a duplex. That was the blueprint you followed.   The same will be true in marriage.

Many a couple has unintentionally followed the blueprint being used by the celebrities. The daily building pattern was laid out for them in the latest super-market rag. Brick by brick and plank by plank they followed the pattern of the beautiful people. But, sad to say, so many of the beautiful people end up with a very ugly marriage. Today's couples may shout, "That is not the kind of marriage we want!" It *will* be that kind of marriage, however, if the current culture provides the blueprint for your marriage. You must choose the correct blueprint for the house you want to build! And you must choose the correct blueprint for the kind of *home* you will build in that *house*.

There *is* a blueprint for a lasting marriage. The foundation and the building material are clearly spelled out. And the instructions to the builders are just as clear. The wife submits a deep sense of respect for her husband. And the husband submits a totally unselfish love for his wife. That sounds simple enough, doesn't it? But let's flesh it out and see how it comes to life, and how it is lived out each day.

"The wife must respect her husband." That is how the Scripture passage concludes. It took the apostle Paul a long time to get to this point, didn't it? He opened the passage by telling wives to *submit*, but we come to the very end of his thoughts before he tells her *what* to submit. That seems so strange, doesn't it? Stranger yet, the Apostle Paul never tells the wife she is to love her husband. He gives the emphatic command, "Husbands, love your wives," but he does

not give this command to the wife. In fact, he, nor any other who recorded the Scriptures, from Genesis to Revelation, tell a wife she is to *love her husband*! What? That's right, nowhere in the Bible is a wife commanded to love her husband.

There is that passage Paul wrote to the young preacher, Titus, where he tells the older women, "to train the younger women to love their husbands and children." The Greek word *love* in this passage is the word most Americans use when they say "love." It is that "I love chocolate pie"..."I'd love to live in that house"... "Man, would I love to have a car like that!" The word love that Paul uses in Titus 2:4 (NIV) means to *find pleasure* in something. It means to *like*! It is not the word John used when he wrote "God so *loved* the world." And it is not the word Paul wrote to the Ephesians when he said, "husbands *love* your wife". The word Paul used when he told Titus that the older women were to teach the younger women to love their husbands is best translated to *like* their husbands. They needed to be taught to find pleasure in or learn how to *like* a husband.

To understand this *liking your husband* bit, we have to understand the culture in which the Apostle Paul had lived. It will be difficult to understand unless we have lived in a culture where marriage was *arranged*. Marriage, for them, did not come about from courtship and choice. It came at the arrangement of mediators and the agreement of the parents.

Do you remember Rebecca in your Bible stories? She was asked by her father, "Will you go with this man?" This man was not her husband-to-be, Isaac. This man was an emissary from Abraham who had been sent to find a wife for his son, Isaac. What Rebecca agreed to was a "sight unseen" marriage. She would return with this messenger to *marry a man she had never met!* Her mother surely had taught her what it means to "*find pleasure* in a husband."

That story in the Bible is from a long time ago, so let me update it with a personal experience. I was sitting in the airport in Cairo, Egypt, when I saw a twin sister to this event. Hundreds of passengers had finally made it through customs when the airport was unexpectedly shut down. A meeting between the heads-of-state of Israel, Egypt, and Jordan had caused the airport to be placed under maximum security. So, there we sat for eight tense hours. All food in the building had been consumed! Restroom facilities were totally overtaxed! And every seat, including most of the floor space, was taken. There was little that could be done except wait. This waiting, however, led to one of my favorite pastimes—learning by observing the people around me.

That's when I saw her. She was a swarthy beauty in her early 20's and she was wearing, what had to be, a wedding dress. In fact, it was a stunning white in direct contrast to all the dark garments that filled the over- crowded waiting area. As she sat there, tears were occasionally slipping down her cheeks. With the frightening and filthy conditions in that airport, I assure you she was not the only person crying. In fact, I heard dozens of babies crying—all at the same time! But, she was crying. That which was to have been a short flight to Jordan had turned into an all-day wait.

Had she actually missed her wedding? Had she not been able to communicate with those who were expecting her? I do not know all the reasons for her tears. Had she been an American bride, however, I would know the greatest reason for her crying. She was leaving her home in Egypt to travel to Jordan to marry *a man she had never met!!!* That young woman had better have been taught to "find pleasure in a husband". That is why the apostle Paul says the older women are to teach the younger women, "to *like*" their husbands. Nowhere, however, does Paul, Peter, Moses, or even Jesus command a woman to *love* her husband.

The first time I came to realize that truth, it left me frustrated. I was frustrated, and just a little bit angry! As a husband I have been commanded "love your wife" and she has not been commanded to love me?! She has a choice? And I have no choice except to obey or disobey the Scriptures? What, in the name of Christianity, can this possibly mean? I am commanded to *love* her, but she is only commanded to *respect* me. Why? I decided to keep my mouth shut on this subject until I could come to understand the *why*.

That "why" was a long time coming. It was years before it became clear. That clarity came through counseling sessions where I heard an oft repeated phrase. Wife after wife had said "Dennis, I love my husband. I just don't respect him." The counselor in me would sit there with a calm, listening demeanor, but the man in me was screaming, "What's she talking about? If she does not respect him, she does not love him"... "I don't care what she says, she does not love him!" Then, it dawned on me! The fog began to lift as I remembered that men and women are not alike! Most women can separate love and respect. They see no inconsistency in "I *love* him. I just don't *respect* him". Men, however, cannot separate love and respect. To them they are Siamese twins and you lose them on the operating table if you try to separate them. For a man to believe he is loved, he must also know that he is respected. He needs to know that the woman he is married to believes he is just a cut above those other fellows. Otherwise, "Why in the world did she marry me?"

God, who created us knows us better than we know ourselves. He knows our weaknesses and our strengths. He knows our needs *and He knows our* temptations. He knows that, in marriage, a woman needs to be given unselfish love, and that a man needs to be shown genuine respect. God knows all this, *but do we?* You can be sure that the *enemy* of God and good knows this. If he can get men to remain as self-centered Mama's boys, never knowing what it is to love unselfishly, they will never know the kind of marriage God had in mind. For him, it will never be "very good!" And if, in the competition between male and female, the Tempter can create in women a sense of disrespect for men they will never experience a successful marriage. Husbands must love their wives and wives must respect their husbands.

The marriage text in Ephesians goes to great lengths to demand and describe the kind of love a husband is to have for his wife. The text begins, however, with the wife, so let's explore that text a little further. If you are a bride-to-be or a wife of many years, know that, at this point, I have removed my shoes and am walking barefoot on very thin ice. This slippery patch of ice must be crossed. It is that patch of ice where I say *"Women are greatly tempted to be disrespectful to men"*. It may be that this disrespect is the result of a male-oriented culture. I do not know all that causes the disrespect, but I have seen it and heard it all too often. And it can begin at a very early age.

Walk with me to the local elementary school. It's recess time and the playground is filled with excessive life. Listen carefully. Did you hear it? There it is again. In fact, two or three voices have joined in. I know that tune, don't you? "Na-na-na-na-naaa-na" "Na-na-na-na-naa-na" Who is singing that dreaded song? If I were a betting man I would say it was a little girl—not a little boy! And, guess what? That is a bet I would usually win. She is not large enough to beat this rotten little boy in a fist fight. But, she doesn't have to! With a volley of words, and that well-worn little chant, she can slice him and dice him and send him home to his mother. With this early training, she can move on up to the minor league. Given enough time, she will be ready for the majors—husband bashing!!

Wait, wait, bride-to-be or experienced wife, please don't put the book down at this point. Go with me a little further until you are firmly convinced of the dangers of disrespect. Go with me to an insurance office in Indianapolis. That is where our oldest daughter worked in the months just before her wedding. The office staff was almost entirely female. Rachel would come home from work with her head spinning from all the negative talk about their husbands, or their boyfriends. She would say, "Dad, all day long they talk down their husbands! You would think they were married to a bunch of idiots." And that talk, obviously, was not uplifting to a marriage. It was that playground chant all over again. It was a boxing bout of words. A jab, jab, here! A right cross there! And then, hopefully, a knockout punch when the entire female staff would break out in laughter. As the day of Rachel's wedding grew closer, one of those acidic conversations grew so painful that she quietly broke into tears. One of the older women, realizing that this time a line had been crossed, stepped over to offer Rachel some consolation. Her conclusion to the conversation was "Oh Rachel, we don't mean all that stuff that we say. It's just something that wives do." As the father of that tender bride-to-be, let me tell you something else those kind of wives do. They get divorced by men who desperately needed their respect!

Dare I push this point any further? Sit down with me in my office and listen in on a conversation. I will not use the real names but I will let you listen in on the real conversation. I had known John and Mary for a long time. I knew them, loved them, and loved their children. John, however, was bailing out on his marriage. The guilt and frustration of an affair had led him to my office and to my counsel as a friend. I listened to this hardworking man, good father, and guilt-ridden husband. As we opened door after door of his mistaken journey, I could not find the door that opened to his affair. In an effort to learn more of his marriage, I said, "John, there's no way you are going to tell me that this woman you are seeing is more beautiful than Mary?" Mary was very physically attractive—she was highly intelligent—and very socially skilled. What of this "other woman?" John became very thoughtful after my question, then broke out in a strange chuckle. He said, "You know, Dennis, this woman I have been seeing is really kinda homely?" No woman wants to be called "homely". Especially by a man with whom she is romantically involved. The revealing statement came when John followed the "homely" with, "But when I'm with her, she makes me feel like I'm somebody!"

So, that was it! When he was with his beautiful, intelligent, and socially skilled wife her constant disrespect made him feel like a "nobody". Then, along came a woman who made him feel like a "somebody". In counseling with John *and* Mary it became evident she was a great practitioner of the "put down". It had now reached the habit level in their marriage. Gratefully, their marriage was salvaged as he learned more about sacrificial love and she learned a lot more about respecting her husband.

Husbands *want* to be loved but they *need* to be respected. Men can not separate love and respect. It is the *respect* that proves to them they are *loved*. That is why the scriptures never commands a woman to love her husband, but speaks with the wisdom of God when it says, the wife must respect her husband. It speaks to *her* great temptation and to *his* great need.

Enough, already, of this talking to the wives! And talking to the wives!! And talking to the wives!! What about the husbands? Surely they are not perfect? God, who knows us so well, knows that men are far from perfect. In fact, at this point the apostle Paul picks up his heaviest gauge shotgun, loads both barrels and takes careful aim. His target? Husbands! The command is about as straightforward as it can be. "Husbands, love your wives!" Yes, I placed an exclamation mark at the end of the sentence. It is there to call our attention to the depths of this love.

The word the Scripture uses here is not our kind of love—"Man, would I love to own a car like that!" It is the word used for God's kind of love—"God so loved the world that he gave His only begotten Son." You really do not have to know any New Testament Greek or understand the difference in the original words to understand the love required of a husband. It is clearly spelled out in the rest of the statement "Husbands love your wives, *just as Christ loved the church* and gave himself up for her." It is that kind of love. Total love! Unselfish love!

When Jesus died on the cross he was not dying to meet *his* needs. He was dying to meet *our* needs. The husband's love, then, is about unselfishly meeting her needs. What about her happiness? Her desires? Her welfare? Her future? Wow! This is where the rubber hits the road and the tires give an uncomfortable squeal. Am I telling you the husband is to love his wife with this kind of love? No, the question is, does the Scripture *command* this kind of love from a husband? The answer is *yes!* It is the love that Jesus had and has for the church.

I thought the scripture teaches that Jesus is *head* of the church and the husband is the *head* of the wife?! It does, but the same verse that announces Him as head of the church declares that He is the Savior of the body. Is the husband, who wants to be the <u>head</u>, willing to be the <u>savior</u>? Will he give himself up to save the marriage?

Experience demonstrates it is usually the *wife* who seeks counsel for the saving of a marriage. Few are the men who willingly reach out for help in breaking the downward spiral. To that few who do seek counsel, I offer my highest commendations! There are others, however, who have gone for counsel only after a desperate appeal from their wife. After that first counseling session, their response is usually, "Never again!" Why? I'm not sure, but it could be a result of many years of subtlety in our upbringing.

In our culture, girls are pointed toward being *desirable*. And boys are pointed toward being *capable*. If this observation has any foundation, having to seek the counsel of another would indicate to a man that he was not *capable* of handling this problem by himself. Is his very manhood threatened by counsel?

There certainly could be another reason many husbands avoid counsel. I hate to mention it because it could be an exceptionally strong indictment of my very own gender. Could it possibly be that men are *self-centered* and prone to *selfishness?* When the apostle Paul commanded the wife to respect her husband was he dealing with a female tendency to be disrespectful? If so, when he commands a husband to love his wife and give himself up for her, is he dealing with the male tendency to be selfish rather than sacrificial? Far be it from me to second-guess an Apostle! He knows the husband needs respect so the wife is commanded to respect him. He knows too, that the wives greatest need is to be loved, so he commands the husband to love his wife as Christ loved the church and gave himself up for her. He is to love her...simply love her...merely love her... love her...love her!

Sound familiar? Well, maybe you have heard the musical <u>Camelot</u>. King Arthur, very typical of many a groom, is nervous over his upcoming marriage to Gwenivere. He had sought counsel and shares the wisdom given to him. It was shared in song: "How to handle a woman? 'There's a way', said the wise old man. 'A way known to every woman, since the whole rig-a-ma-role began.' 'Do I flatter her?', I begged him answer. 'Do I threaten or plead?' 'Do I brood? Or play the gay romancer?' Said he, smiling, 'No, indeed.' 'How to handle a woman, mark thee well, I will tell you sir. The way to handle a woman is to love her...simply love her...merely love her...love her!' "

There may be husbands who were moved by that scene. There may be many, however, who have never seen or read Camelot. Whatever the case, know that the Scriptures are older and wiser than *the wise old man*. And the love the Scripture commands of a husband is not *simply,* or *merely,* but is *completely*!! It is that sacrificial love of Christ that contained not one ounce of selfishness. But *knowing* sacrificial love is required in a marriage is no guarantee that it will be the kind of love *brought* to the marriage. There *is* that male temptation to be self-centered, isn't there? Maybe this can be blamed on our Mothers. "Momma cooked for me...Momma made my bed...Momma did the wash for me. I'm going to get married, and marry me another Momma." Obviously I do not want to be hard on a mother's love. Nor do I wish to be harsh with myself or any other man who is reading this book. But men have to face the fact that they have a strong tendency to be self-centered!

I remember at least two marriages where the young husbands thought it was great that their wives got to go to the gym three nights a week and watch *them* play basketball!! They were totally oblivious to the needs of their wives. There has been no opportunity to follow those two marriages down through the years. Had there been opportunity, I am sure I would have observed some rocky years. I am sure, also, if either of those husbands decided to end their marriages, it would have been because of the kind of *wife* they had gotten. It would not occur to them it was only because of the kind of *husband* they had been!

The unselfish love the Scriptures demand of a husband does not rest on *his* needs being met. It does expect him to question whether

her needs are being met. *Remember,* it is the kind of love Christ had. *Remember* He did not die on the cross to meet *His* needs. He was there to meet *ours. Remember* the husband is to love his wife as Christ loved the church and gave Himself up for her. Have I used the word *remember* too often? I can assure you a husband had best not forget these words from the Scriptures.

A *loving* husband and a *respectful* wife is the Biblical blueprint for marriage. Let me try to "flesh out" this blueprint, by offering a direct contrast. I say "flesh out" because the following story is true, only the names have been changed to protect the guilty. Well, I will not change the names—I simply will not use them.

He was gainfully employed in a job that paid an average salary. His family, however, lived in a very small three room house with an outdoor toilet. Had it not been for assistance from her parents, his wife and children would not always have the food and clothing they needed. Despite *their* needs, *his* needs seem to be amply met. He had an automobile, a pickup truck, and a motorcycle. And, despite the fact they had only a postage stamp yard, he had a small tractor just for puttering around. He had come from a farm family, so surely he also needed to have a tractor. His wife and his family had many needs! He had many toys! So much for sacrificial love!

Now, for the rest of the story—that part about respecting your husband. If she had any respect for him it was never displayed. It is doubtful she had respect for men—period! Maybe for her father, but I never saw it venture beyond that. Respect a man? Why? She could work at manual labor as hard and as long as any man. She walked like a man and she talked like a man. Long before it was vogue for women to wear slacks, she was seldom seen in anything except blue jeans or bib overalls. She would roll up those overlong trousers and would shake the ashes from her cigarette into the cuffs of those blue jeans! Just like the best of men! She was the antithesis of "wife respect your husband". And he was in reverse gear on "husband, love your wife…give yourself up for her."

Can you possibly imagine a day in the life of this inappropriate couple? He dreads the work day coming to an end. When his work ends he must go home. Home? Dread the thought! She has been home all day long, loading the verbal missiles she will release soon after he walks through the door. You can be sure the tension in the evening meal would make for an indigestion special. Her recall of the broken knob on the door, or yesterday's clothes left in the floor will justify the disrespect she has in store for him. And he, who *has* to eat, has no desire to make this mealtime one minute longer than it needs to be. He had to get out of this house! So, as soon as his last swallow, will he rush out to drive his car or his truck? Or will it be a ride on his motorcycle? Or dare he be bold enough to putter around in the yard with his tractor? That will, after all, still be close enough to the house to be in ear shot!

Oh, for a day in the life of a woman who still holds to the disrespect of a playground schoolgirl and her "Nah-na-na-na-naa-nah!" And, oh, the misery of a man who has never grown beyond the self-centeredness of a mamma's-boy with all his toys. A marriage like this will surely end in divorce. And it did!

Could the marriage principles of Ephesians 5 have salvaged this marriage? I think so. Think with me in a little game of "What if". What if he had ceased being a spoiled little boy with all of his toys? And, what if the money that was spent for *his* self-indulgence was now spent to unselfishly meet *her* needs! What if this became *his* consistent, even constant, pattern of being an "Unselfish husband" to this "Disrespectful wife?" Am I being naïve to believe that her respect for him would begin to grow? I do not know how long it would take, but I believe it would happen! Don't you? How could she continue being disrespectful in the face of such unselfish love? Unless she was a psychological basket case or a spiritual reprobate, I believe the proper response would have begun. I even believe respect would, eventually, become *her* consistent and constant pattern.

Let's flip the coin over and play a little "What if" on the other side. What if her everyday resistive spirit began to soften And what if her masculine image began to change, until she no longer was in competition with her man, and even became attractive to him? What if, above all, the seizing of every opportunity to berate and humiliate him ceased? What if her conduct began to take on a likeness of respect? Even a likeness to "Wives, submit to your husbands as to the Lord!" Once again, am I being naïve to believe it would bring a change in him? How long before it would become apparent to him that she had placed it all in his hands? Her welfare…her happiness… her future all centered in him! Would not his self-centeredness begin to crack in the presence of this genuine respect. Unless he was badly damaged psychologically or totally deficient spiritually, I believe there would be a proper response.

Unselfish love would call for respect, and genuine respect would get the attention of an unselfish love. The more he totally loves her, the easier it is for her to respect him. The more she respects him, the easier it becomes for him to love her. The more she respects him, the more his unselfish attention is turned to her….. *and* the cycle goes on! And on! And on!

Here's what I suggest. In fact, I suggest it to every bride and groom who sits before me in pre-marital counsel. I suggest that they turn to Ephesians 5:21-33 and read it. I suggest they read it every day. I suggest they read it corporately, and I suggest they read it individually each morning and each evening. Read it each morning and evening of every day. Every day! And every day! I want it read until they finally say, "That stupid preacher . We *know* what it says!!!" I trust it would be read until it finally becomes, not just a passage in *His* book, but a thought process in *their* minds. I would like it etched there so deeply that the first time her words to him takes on a certain disdainful tone…or when there is that facial expression that requires no words to say, "what an idiot"…or when she becomes a major player in the game of husband bashing…I want this Scripture to chime in with, "I don't know what you think you are doing young lady, but *that is not respect!!*"

Or that first time those of us who are men revert to a momma's boy with all *his* little toys and forgets about *her* needs…..I hope this

Scripture will nail our hides to the wall and clearly say, "What in the world were you thinking? You were not thinking about *her* needs, were you? You were thinking about *yourself*. Admit it! You were just a selfish little boy who needs to grow up and become man-sized in your love for your wife".

For those who are about to say "I do," this pattern of "Wives respect your husbands and husbands love your wife as Christ loved the Church," is the most vital marriage advice *you will ever be given*. And to those of us who have already said "I do" and are doing and will keep on doing, this Scripture must always be the *pattern* for our doing.

Whether bride and groom or husband and wife, we will, then, be building on *the* blueprint. The *blueprint* from the one who conducted the very first marriage ceremony. The One who created male and female and declared it to be *"very good"*. Ours will become a marriage that is not dominated by the "I do what?" question. But it will become a marriage that loudly shouts "I do!". I do pledge myself to follow the Biblical blueprint for marriage.

No, it will not be a fairy-tale marriage. You will not feed on sugar plums as you float through life on a fluffy pink cloud. Even with the Biblical blueprint for marriage, there will still be "Better and Worse, "Richer and Poorer", and "Sickness and Health." But we surely know, that the Architect of Marriage has taken all this into account. With the instruction from His marriage manual, and with our permission for His involvement in our daily details, we will begin to see what He meant when He said it was *"very good!"* I believe that pronouncement of *"very good"* is a synonym for *"They all lived happily ever after"*, don't you?

All together, then, let's willingly and emphatically say, "I do!" No ifs, ands, buts, or whats about it…**"I DO!!!"**

I. HOLY MATRIMONY

In the very beginning marriage was presented as one man, one woman, and God. In contrast to secular patterns of domestic partnership discuss the value of Biblical marriage in regard to

- The happiness of the couple

- The stability of a family

- The value to civilization

God, who created marriage, said to "leave Father and Mother and cleave unto his wife, and the two will become one flesh". (KJV) Take a serious look at

LEAVING! The five major causes of divorce are money, sex, faith, communication, and family Do either of you see your Father or Mother as a strength in your marriage? Or a source of interference? Would they, in any way, welcome a divorce?

Can you see a balance between "Honor your Father and Mother" and "leave your Father and Mother".

CLEAVING! The Bible urges Christians to be of the "same mind and judgment". If that is taught generally, it is certainly essential for a husband and wife. Are there areas of your life that are united in the same mind and judgment? Areas in which you disagree? Areas that are open for discussion?

<u>UNITING</u>! It's obvious that the declaration "one flesh" is a reference to sexual union, without which a marriage is never considered consummated. Are there areas other than physical that need to be consummated before there is real oneness?

MENTALLY?

EMOTIONALLY?

SPIRITUALLY?

How are you doing in these areas?

<u>Notes on valued impressions from your discussion:</u>

_____

_____

_____

_____

_____

THIS WOMAN THIS MAN

Is it true that we do not usually enjoy being around people who differ from us? Are their friends from years gone by that have simply disappeared? Why? Was it because you now have little in common? They are different? You are different? Discuss the why and what of those dissolved friendships.

Marriage, however, is a *commitment* to live the rest of your life with someone who is different from you! What are some of the ways you perceive as male and female differences?

PHYSICALLY?

MENTALLY?

EMOTIONALLY?

SOCIALLY?

SPIRITUALLY?

Just for the sake of a spirited discussion, and knowing that the word "always" is always argumentative, fill in the blanks:

WHY DO MEN ALWAYS? _____

_____

WHY DO WOMEN ALWAYS? _____

_____

Repeat this list as often a necessary to come to the realization that male and female are not alike! Affirm the maxim "If you accept the privilege of being sexually different, you accept the responsibility of differences that are personal, social, or emotional."

Notes on valued impressions from your discussion:

_____

_____

_____

_____

_____

_____

_____

_____

_____

THIS WOMAN THIS MAN

What are some of your character traits, habits, or daily patterns that could be stressful to a marriage?

1. _____
2. _____
3. _____
4. _____
5. _____
6. _____
etc.

Are there things about your spouse you would like for them to change? (Remember, if you cannot discuss these things now, you will not discuss them later. You will argue about them later but you will not discuss them).

Are there some things you would be willing to change in order to have a better marriage?

Are there matters you are unwilling to give up for fear of losing your personhood?

What changes do you anticipate because of marriage?

Notes on valued impressions from your discussion:

_____

_____

_____

_____

_____

_____

_____

_____

_____

BETTER OR WORSE

Have you known couples who have faced some very serious problems in their marriages? Did those couples divorce? Or did their marriages only grow stronger?

For those who divorced were there changes one, or both could or should have made? (You do not need to discuss their names, but you do need to be very specific in your discussion).

What do you perceive to be the key or keys to those couples who grew stronger through difficulties in their marriage?

What do you believe your response would be to the situations they faced?

What are some of the worst scenarios you believe a marriage could face? And what do you believe your course of action would be?

Notes on valued impressions from your discussion:

_____

_____

_____

_____

_____

_____

_____

_____

_____

_____

RICHER OR POORER?

What is the financial background of your family?

Were they fairly wealthy or reasonable poor? Were there unemployments and seasons of little or no income? Were there luxury cruises, lengthy vacations and extensive travel? Were there foreclosures or bankruptcies?

On the scale below, place a check mark to indicate your family's balance between two financial extremes.

GROOM'S FAMILY
SAVERS ---- ---- ---- ---- ---- ---- ---- ---- SPENDERS

BRIDE'S FAMILY
SAVERS ---- ---- ---- ---- ---- ---- ---- ---- SPENDERS

YOUR LIFESTYLE
SAVER ---- ---- ---- ---- ---- ---- ---- ---- SPENDER

Have you ever made a list of things you consider _necessities_ and things you consider _luxuries_? How well would you do when you compared lists? Do either of you bring outstanding debts to your marriage? Student loans? Auto loans? Credit card debt, etc.???

Have either of you visited a third-world country? Supported a needy or homeless child? Tithed to a church? Served in a non-profit organization? And what do you think is a fair tip to those who serve you in a restaurant? Do you have a budget or intend to develop a family budget? And who will pay the bills? Is there any question about "yours", "mine", and "ours"?

Notes on valued impressions from your discussion:

_____

_____

_____

_____

_____

_____

_____

_____

_____

SICKNESS OR HEALTH?

Have you known marriages where serious health issues were handled in such a manner that you were inspired by the love that was evident?

Are there other cases where the results were disastrous and your image of marriage was lessened?

What is your family health history? Heart disease? Obesity? Cancer? Disabilities?

Many health issues are subject to dietary regulations. Are there dietary regimens either of you expect to follow in your home?

VEGAN
VEGETARIAN
CARNIVORE
MEAT, MEAT – MORE MEAT

How are you doing in matters that are universally accepted as negatives to good health:

ALCOHOL	EXERCISE:
Socially?_____	Couch potato?_____
Daily?_____	Some exercise?_____
Addicted?_____	Regular workout?_____
Never?_____	Runner?_____

Have you ever or are you now using drugs? _____

What do you think your response would be to a chronic, debilitating medical condition in yourself?
Or in your mate? How do you usually respond to illness or pain?

Notes on valued impressions from your discussion:

_____

_____

_____

_____

_____

_____

I PROMISE YOU MY LOVE

Do you believe the feelings come from the doing, or the doing comes from the feelings? (Do you need to review this chapter?)

Have you ever, or do you now, have feelings of attachment to an inanimate object? Car? Home? Sports? Memorabilia? Stuffed toy? Why?

Have you ever "loved" a pet? Is there a difference between loving and liking?

How are you doing in those Biblical areas that describe real love? Give it a checkmark check up!

	NAILING IT	USUALLY	WORKING ON IT
Patient	_____	_____	_____
Kind	_____	_____	_____
Not envious	_____	_____	_____
Bragging	_____	_____	_____
Proud	_____	_____	_____
Rudeness	_____	_____	_____
Selfish	_____	_____	_____
Anger	_____	_____	_____
Vengeful	_____	_____	_____
Judgmental	_____	_____	_____
Celebration	_____	_____	_____
Protects	_____	_____	_____
Trusts	_____	_____	_____
Hopeful	_____	_____	_____
Perseverance	_____	_____	_____

Take time for some face-to-face sharing on this list.

Notes on valued impressions from your discussion.

_____

_____

_____

_____

PRESENTATION OF THE RINGS

The wedding ceremony calls the ring "a token of the promise made". Is the word "token" too small a word? Discuss what the ring means to you. Do you think it appropriate that the ring, the most frequently used symbol of marriage, should be placed on the finger of a hand? Think of how many deeds of the hand can be the "doing" that expresses or develops your love. Dishes? Mowing? Making the bed? Etc.

Do you view your ring as an announcement to others, or as a reminder to you? Is there strength and protection in both of these views?

Are there other ways or objects to remind you and those around you of your spouse?

Inasmuch as the ring was presented in the name of the Father, the Son, and the Holy Spirit, God is to be a distinct part of the marriage. Do you have plans for:

DAILY DEVOTIONS

CHURCH ATTENDANCE

PRAYER

Notes on valued impressions from your discussion:

_____

_____

_____

_____

_____

_____

_____

_____

_____

<u>PROCLAMATION OF MARRIAGE</u>

Are there husbands or wives you have known who have been outstanding in their marriage? A man who approached that "ideal husband" status? A woman you looked to as a model of an "ideal wife" What can you learn, or what have you learned from these role models?

And those marriages that have been disastrous? Have they shown you some pitfalls to be avoided? What are those pitfalls?

Have you discussed some of the daily chores that belong to the husband? The wife? To be shared? Do you need to make a list?

The first marriage was one man, one woman, and God. That Biblical marriage was instructed to result in oneness! How do you think that best achieved.

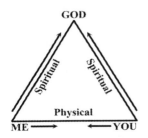

Take a look at this graph and determine what your marriage pattern would be.

Isn't it true that the initial move toward "oneness" is physical? And isn't it also true that this does not bring total oneness?

Could it be that the ultimate unity will be spiritual? If the husband is drawn closer to God and the wife is growing closer to God, isn't it true that the distance between them will diminish? The closer they become to God the closer they become to each other. They will become that ideal marriage—one man, one woman, and God! Surely they will *live happily ever after!*

Notes on valued impressions from your discussion:

_____

_____

_____

_____

BLUEPRINT FOR MARRIAGE

What kind of Blueprint for marriage have you inherited from your parents? Has there been love and respect? Is it your desire for these traits to be seen in your marriage?

The wife is to respect her husband—but disrespect is not exclusively a female trait. Discuss some of the following ways disrespect is shown:

Tone of voice! It is not what is said as much as how it is said. Demonstrate to each other the tone you consider disrespectful. Now that you know that tone, make it a point to avoid it in your marriage.

Body language! There are times when disrespect is shown without a word being spoken. Can you share with each other some of this lethal body language?

Pet Phrases! One of the most common disrespectful sign-off's is, "Whatever!" It is usually spoken while exiting the room. Can you make a list of other "gotcha" words?

It is obvious that both husband and wife are to love each other. The need for that to be expressed has become so common that the phrase, "Love ya", has replaced "Goodbye" as the parting words in a telephone conversation. Discuss some ways you can assure this phrase has real meaning.

The specific kind of love required of a husband is unselfish, sacrificial love. But surely, husbands are not the only marriage partners capable of selfishness. Can you identify some "danger zones" that stand in your way of being an unselfish, sacrificial lover?

Play a game of "what if". What if he flirts or appears to love someone else, do you, then, have permission to be disrespectful to him? Or, if you are disrespectful to him does he have permission to love someone else? Maybe we have not regarded disrespect as a serious offense. Why not discuss this "what if." And which is more important...love or respect?

Have you read Ephesians 5:21–33? Often? Memorized it? Or know it well enough to hear it speak to you when you wander off the path. Are you fully convinced it is the solid foundation for a lasting marriage?

Notes on valued impressions from your discussion:

_____

_____

_____

_____

_____

_____

_____

_____

_____